LIFT AS YOU CLIMB

To wise activist Shelley Washburne Masar,
who introduced me to Ella Baker
—P. H. P.

Dedicated to the SNCC movement facilitators
and the many other people of the '60s
who took action beyond their words
to battle racism and ignorance.—R. G. C.

MARGARET K. McELDERRY BOOKS
An imprint of Simon & Schuster Children's Publishing Division
1230 Avenue of the Americas, New York, New York 10020
Text copyright © 2020 by Patricia Hruby Powell
Illustrations copyright © 2020 by R. Gregory Christie
All rights reserved, including the right of reproduction in whole or in part in any form.
MARGARET K. McELDERRY BOOKS is a trademark of Simon & Schuster, Inc.
For information about special discounts for bulk purchases, please contact
Simon & Schuster Special Sales at 1-866-506-1949 or business@simonandschuster.com.
The Simon & Schuster Speakers Bureau can bring authors to your live event.
For more information or to book an event, contact the Simon & Schuster Speakers Bureau
at 1-866-248-3049 or visit our website at www.simonspeakers.com.
Book design by Lauren Rille
The text for this book was set in Clarendon.
The illustrations for this book were hand painted in Acryla Gouache paints.
Manufactured in China
0320 SCP
First Edition
10 9 8 7 6 5 4 3 2 1
Library of Congress Cataloging-in-Publication Data
Names: Powell, Patricia Hruby, 1951– author. | Christie, R. Gregory, 1971– illustrator.
Title: Lift as you climb : the story of Ella Baker / Patricia Hruby Powell ;
Illustrated by R. Gregory Christie.
Other titles: Story of Ella Baker
Description: First edition. | New York : Margaret K. McElderry Books, [2019] | Audience: Ages 4–8.
Identifiers: LCCN 2017043916 (print) | ISBN 9781534406230 (hardcover) |
ISBN 9781534406247 (eBook)
Subjects: LCSH: Baker, Ella, 1903–1986—Juvenile literature. | Civil rights workers—United States—
Biography—Juvenile literature. | African American women civil rights workers—Biography—
Juvenile literature.
Classification: LCC E185.97.B214 P68 2019 (print) | DDC 323.092 [B]—dc23
LC record available at https://lccn.loc.gov/2017043916

LIFT AS YOU CLIMB

The Story of Ella Baker

Patricia Hruby Powell   R. Gregory Christie

Margaret K. McElderry Books
New York London Toronto Sydney New Delhi

Under a bright North Carolina sun
Ella rode to church
with Granddaddy
and Mama.

When Granddaddy Mitchell stood to preach
Ella sat in the deacon's chair
legs ruler straight
ears soaking up his strong voice.

He preached
    Give to others.
He preached
    Join together.
He spoke
    Freedom.

He asked

WHAT DO YOU HOPE TO ACCOMPLISH?

After church
at Granddaddy's farm—
the farm he and Grandma worked as slaves—
the farm they toiled on like mules after Emancipation
till they bought and owned it—
where Ella played catch-ball
with her cousins until Grandma said,
 Dinnertime.
And afterwards,
 LISTEN.

Back when we was slaves,
Master said, Bet, you marry light-skinned Carter.
I said, No how!
Master—also my daddy—
made me plow the swamp
to break me.

After turning the muck
I went and jumped the broom—married
proud dark Mitchell, your granddaddy—
and danced all night long.

Ella drank up that story
till it filled her bones.

She LISTENED
to neighbors
tell about chopping cotton.
Many still lived in shacks,
worked white people's land
like her grandparents had
back in slave days.

On their land
her grandparents raised vegetables,
hogs, and cows.
On their land
they built a church
and a school.

Church said
    Help your neighbor.
Mama said
    Lift as you climb.

When Ella was about ten
Mama said,
   Ella, help the neighbors.
Ella rounded up
the motherless children,
dragged 'em home,
dunked 'em,
scrubbed 'em,
dressed 'em in clean clothes,
returned them to their
grateful daddy.

Ella harvested peas.
After her family ate their fill
she took a peck of peas to the
neighbors.
When strangers came over
Ella'd stoke the fire,
warm the food,
serve it.

At fourteen
Ella set off for boarding school
in Raleigh—
high school and college at Shaw University—
top of her class.
Worked as a waitress
to pay her way.
After she graduated
Ella moved
to New York City.

She asked herself,

WHAT DO I HOPE TO ACCOMPLISH?

She would lift as she climbed.

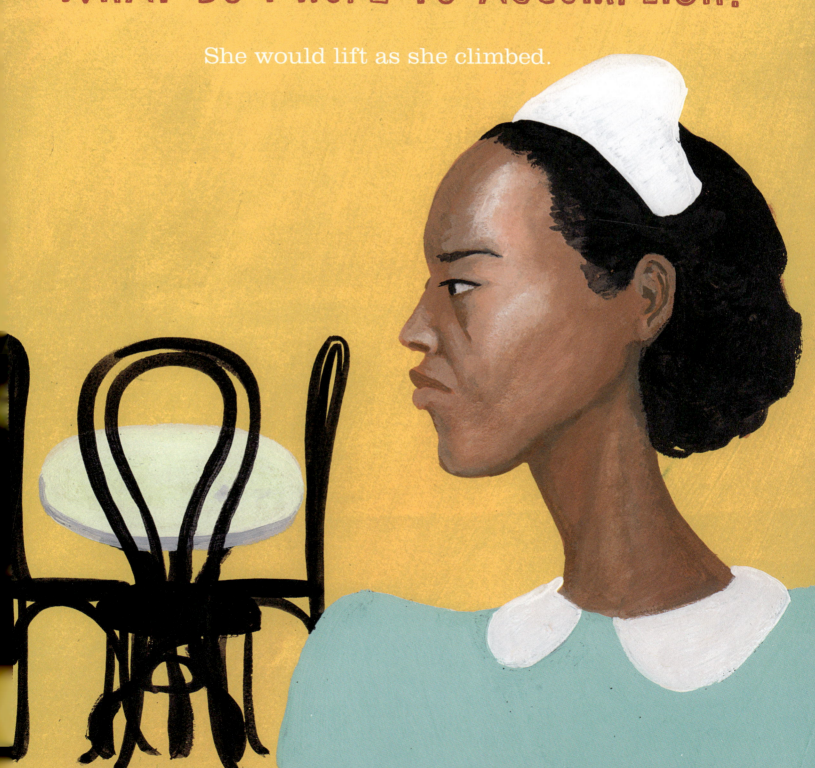

She joined voices that demanded:
Don't Buy Where You Can't Work.

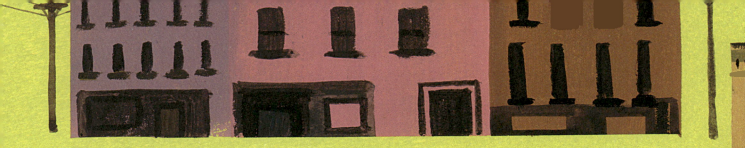

Negroes needed jobs.
White shop owners needed
Negroes to buy from their shops
or they'd close.
Without jobs—without money—
Negroes couldn't buy from white shops.
Ella and other colored people
told the shop owners so.
Some whites hired a few blacks.
They needed each other.
Ella fought for that step toward justice.

She fought for rights.
She fought for her people.
She got a job with the NAACP.
The N-double-A-C-P
raised money to fight racial injustice
in the courts
by selling memberships—
and registering voters.

The NAACP focused on finding members
in the Negro elite—
preachers, doctors, businessmen.
But Ella had a different idea.
She'd find a church.
Get herself invited.
Talk at Sunday service.
Make friends with everyday people—
middle-class maids, shop workers,
and poor sharecroppers—
not just the elite—
and ask,

WHAT DO YOU HOPE TO ACCOMPLISH?

She LISTENED in Mims, Florida—
    Our school principal
    asked for teachers' pay
    equal to white teachers' pay.
Whites dynamited his house.
Killed him.
Ella mourned, then said,
    You want equal pay for Negroes?
    Register to vote.
    Choose your representative.
    They will LISTEN to your complaint.
    That representative will fight
    for the Negro.

All over the South
Ella made speeches
about freedom—
voting—
rights—
words straight from her heart
to the hearts of her audience.
Then she'd ask

WHAT DO YOU HOPE TO ACCOMPLISH?

In one Virginia town, people objected to police brutality.
Why'd the police beat Negroes
when they hadn't committed a crime?

Another town wanted better teachers' salaries and school buses.

Another—use of city parks and playgrounds.

They wanted fair treatment.
But the Negro middle class resisted
joining the NAACP—
and getting the vote.
Why anger their white bosses?
Risk their jobs? Their comforts?
Why risk being hungry?

Ella told this story—
    Across the tracks
    the poor live in filth and get diseases.
    Those diseases hop those
    itty-bitty tracks
    and infect you.

That made sense to the middle class.
All Negroes were in this together.
They'd have to risk angering their bosses.

Ella and her new friends—
workers, partners, believers—
mostly women—
walked into
bar-and-grills,
schools,
beer gardens,
bootblack parlors.
She was always the poised lady,
always Miss Baker
posing the question,

The people wanted
FREEDOM.

Martin Luther King Jr.
      and one hundred men—
mostly preachers—
and Ella
worked together
for black freedom.
They formed the
Southern
Christian
Leadership
Conference.

Churches worked with preachers at the top
handing down knowledge
from the pulpit
to the flock.
That's how these preachers wanted to work now—
like their churches did,
from the top down.

Ella worked from the bottom up—
from the grass roots.
She wanted people
to solve their own problems
like her mother taught her—
    lifting as she climbed.

But the powerful men weren't used to women working
in their inner circle.

Ella LISTENED to the people,
then raised their questions
with the preachers.

Shouldn't we harness the power
of black women as leaders?
Shouldn't we train local leaders?
Shouldn't we create education programs?

She challenged Reverend King with her ideas.
Rather than just the elite
and the middle class—
what about the poorest?
What about the people at the bottom?

Dr. King didn't always agree with Ella.
But he respected her.
He said,
    Ella must head up
    our new organization—the SCLC—
    to register voters,
    stand up to the whites.

His order came from the top down.
Ella thought he should ask—
not command.
Still, she agreed—
for the cause.
For the Freedom Movement,
she'd empower people to take action.
She'd register voters.

Then something amazing happened.
Negro students
sat at "whites-only" lunch counters.
They wanted to be served a hamburger
alongside white people
in the store where they bought school supplies—
in Greensboro, Nashville,
Atlanta, Durham.
Sit-ins exploded throughout the South.

Ella had never been so excited.

She brought the students together
at a conference at Shaw University.
She wanted them to organize.
A united swell of voices was more powerful
than individual voices.
They asked her advice.

Always the teacher
she asked them

WHAT DO YOU HOPE TO ACCOMPLISH?

They wanted to register voters.
They wanted to stage sit-ins.
They named themselves
Student Nonviolent Coordinating Committee—
SNCC—*snick*.

Students staged sit-ins.
Some got whipped. Or spat on.
They sat quietly—responding with nonviolence.

Many were jailed.

Ella LISTENED
and comforted them—
brought toothbrushes
and soap to their cells.
She advised them—
    Lift as you climb.

The students ventured back into the fight
armed with Ella's wisdom.

Tennessee tenant farmers—
poor Negroes working for white plantation owners—
hungry and bone-tired from overwork,
tried to register to vote.
White bosses
evicted them from their shacks.
Beat them for being bold.
Now the sharecroppers lived in tents.

The students asked them,
WHAT DO YOU HOPE TO ACCOMPLISH?

They wanted justice.
They wanted the vote.
They wanted to be treated like citizens.

Ella worked alongside the students
when they rode in battered school buses
and commercial buses.
Testing the new integration laws
by breaking old Jim Crow laws,
they sat in "whites-only" seats.
They came South to help
desegregate.
In Alabama, the buses were
fire-bombed.
Students were
beaten,
jailed.
Those Freedom Riders of 1961
woke up the nation.

Ella had helped plan the rides.

She advised the students
in meetings,
on car trips,
over ice cream sundaes,
at night sharing tiny beds
as the students brainstormed,
connected, struggled
to become their own leaders—

many of them women
when it was new
to be a woman
leading.

Ella said,

WE ARE NOT FIGHTING FOR THE FREEDOM OF THE NEGRO ALONE, BUT FOR THE FREEDOM OF THE HUMAN SPIRIT.

To her last days, Ella fought for freedom,
lifting as she climbed.
The seeds she sowed all her life
continue to bear fruit today.
She said,

THE STRUGGLE FOR RIGHTS
DIDN'T START YESTERDAY
AND HAS TO CONTINUE
UNTIL IT IS WON.

Ella Josephine Baker was born on December 13, 1903, in Norfolk, Virginia. Her parents were Blake Baker and Georgianna "Anna" Ross Baker. Ella spent summers on the farm of her grandparents, Mitchell and Elizabeth Ross, in Littleton, North Carolina. The Bakers moved to a Littleton neighborhood near the Ross farm when Ella was seven. Blake Baker, the son of slaves, worked as a waiter on the commuter ferry between Norfolk and Washington DC and came home when he could. Anna Ross Baker, a working member of the North Carolina (Black Baptist) Convention, saw to it that Ella was a "proper young lady raised in the church."

The Black Baptist school, Shaw Academy in North Carolina, where Ella went to both high school and university, was founded to help educate members of what W. E. B. Du Bois called the "Talented Tenth"—the highly educated black population that would lead the black race in progress.

Ella Baker, or Miss Baker as she was invariably called, was an anomaly in the Freedom Movement. As an attractive, eloquent, and poised lady with radical views, she fought the sexism that was so prevalent at that time (including in the SCLC and in the NAACP, where she was hired, or "drafted"). In the SNCC years, she was the senior advisor, still radical and poised. While choosing her battles with Jim Crow, she never fit the stereotype of a rabble-rouser.

Ella kept her personal life to herself. Few people knew she was married for twenty-one years to civil rights worker T. J. Roberts, but did not take his name. Later in life, she took over the raising of her niece, Jacqueline Brockington, her sister's child.

Ella Baker was a colleague and advisor to Martin Luther King Jr. She worked alongside generations of civil rights workers, including W. E. B. Du Bois, Thurgood Marshall, Stokely Carmichael, Rosa Parks, and Fannie Lou Hamer. She was the mentor of younger civil rights workers, including Bob Moses, John Lewis, Julian Bond, Marian Wright Edelman, Diane Nash, and many others.

Nonviolent resistance as practiced by SNCC members (but not by Ella

Baker) was modeled after the teaching of Gandhi and based on love and the love of God, specifically to "absorb evil, all the while persisting in love."

Anyone who worked for the Black Freedom Movement (or for the Women's Movement) in the 1960s knew Ella Baker. But because she worked behind the scenes and didn't care about the spotlight, nor believed in following a charismatic figure or being followed, she is less known than she should be.

ADDITIONAL INFORMATION

Some of the organizations that Ella worked with were:

YNCL: Young Negroes Cooperative League, established in 1930, developed local consumer cooperatives, such as food co-ops, throughout the country. If they bought as a group rather than as individuals, they could get a better deal.

WPA: Works Progress Administration or Work Projects Administration, created during the depths of the Great Depression by order of President Franklin D. Roosevelt in 1935 as part of the New Deal, employed workers to build roads, bridges, schools, and museums, and to help beautify the nation with waterworks, fairgrounds, playgrounds, and so much more.

NAACP: National Association for the Advancement of Colored People, was established in 1909. Its stated mission remains: "to ensure the political, educational, social, and economic equality of rights of all persons and to eliminate race-based discrimination."

YWCA: Young Women's Christian Association, established in 1858 as a group of women working for social justice to advocate for women's leadership, peace, justice, human rights, and sustainable development.

SCLC: Southern Christian leadership Conference, established in 1957, has promoted the church's participation in the Civil Rights Movement and for a time was headed by Reverend Martin Luther King Jr.

SNCC (spoken as "snick"): Student Nonviolent Coordinating Committee, established in 1960, was active in the Civil Rights Movement. Its main actions were to register Negro voters and to practice nonviolent direct action such as sit-ins.

TIME LINE OF ELLA BAKER'S LIFE

1903 (December 13): Born in Norfolk, VA, to Georgianna "Anna" Ross Baker and Blake Baker

1911: Baker family moves to Littleton, NC, near the Ross family farm

1918–1927: Attends boarding school at Shaw Academy and college at Shaw University, Raleigh, NC

1927: Moves to New York City, works as waitress

1929: The Great Depression begins, hitting Harlem and the black community hard

1929–1931: Works as journalist at *American West Indian News* and on the staff at *Negro National News*

1931–1941: National director of Young Negroes Cooperative League (YNCL); joins the staff of the New York Public Library and develops consumer education and literacy programs for young mothers; publicity director of National Negro Congress (NNC); works for Works Progress Administration (WPA)

1935: "The Bronx Slave Market," an article coauthored with Marvel Cook, is published in *The Crisis*

1941: Joins NAACP as assistant field director; becomes director of branches in 1943

1954: US Supreme Court decision in *Brown v. Board of Education of Topeka* declares segregated schools inherently unequal; the fight begins to apply the ruling and to integrate schools

1957: Helps establish Southern Christian Leadership Conference (SCLC)

1960 (February): Sit-ins begin in Greensboro at a Woolworth's lunch counter.
(April): Helps found Student Nonviolent Coordinating Committee (SNCC)

1961: Summer Freedom Rides begin

1963–1986: Remains active in "the cause"

1965: President Johnson signs Voting Rights Act, fortifying the Fifteenth Amendment. The act aims to overcome legal barriers to African American voting at the state and local levels.

1986 (December 13, her birthday): Dies in New York City at the age of eighty-three.

BIBLIOGRAPHY

Books, Films, Articles
Baker, Ella. "Bigger Than a Hamburger." *Southern Patriot* 18 (June 1960). http://www.historyisaweapon.com/defcon1/bakerbigger.html

Baker, Ella, and Marvel Cooke. "Bronx Slave Market." *The Crisis,* November 1935.

Cantarow, Ellen. "Ella Baker: Organizing for Civil Rights." *In Moving the Mountain: Women Working for Social Change,* 52–93. NY: Feminist Press/McGraw Hill, 1980.

Grant, Joanne. *Ella Baker: Freedom Bound.* NY: John Wiley, 1998.

Grant, Joanne. *Fundi: The Story of Ella Baker*. A film by Joanne Grant. NY: Icarus Films, 1981.

Moye, J. Todd. *Ella Baker: Community Organizer of the Civil Rights Movement*. Rowman & Littlefield, 2013.

Ransby, Barbara. *Ella Baker and the Black Freedom Movement: A Radical Democratic Vision*. Chapel Hill: UNC Press, 2003.

Zinn, Howard. *SNCC: The New Abolitionists*. Boston: Beacon Press, 1964.

Interviews, Oral Histories

Baker, Ella, "Interview Excerpts—Ella Baker," interview by Emily Stoper. Harvard University dissertation 1968, Carlson Publishing, 1989. Originally published in *The Student Nonviolent Coordinating Committee*. http://www.crmvet.org/nars/bakere.htm

Baker, Ella, interview by Sue Thrasher and Casey Hayden, April 19, 1977, G-0008 Southern Oral History Program Collection #4007.

Travis, Brenda, interview by Bruce Hartford, February 2007. http://www.crmvet.org/nars/travisb.htm